Books by Bonnie J. Morris

Jewish History
Lubavitcher Women in America
The High School Scene in the Fifties

Women's History
Women's History For Beginners
The Feminist Revolution

Lesbian Fiction
The Question of Sabotage
52 Pickup
Sappho's Bar and Grill
Sappho's Overhead Projector

One-Woman Play/Memoir
Revenge of the Women's Studies Professor

Lesbian Nonfiction
The Eden Built by Eves
Girl Reel
The Bar Notebooks
The Disappearing L

Children's Book
Big and Strong...I Belong!

Chapbooks
The Schoolgirl's Atlas
Sixes and Sevens

Earlier Households

Earlier Households

Bonnie J. Morris

HEADMISTRESS PRESS

ISBN 978-1-7358236-1-4

Cover art © 1976 by Donna Gottschalk. *Self-portrait in Maine.*
Cover & book design by Mary Meriam.

PUBLISHER
Headmistress Press
60 Shipview Lane
Sequim, WA 98382
Telephone: 917-428-8312
Email: headmistresspress@gmail.com
Website: headmistresspress.blogspot.com

For the divine muses in these enduring households:

Shannon and Julie
Laurie and Lynette
Lillian and Phyllis
Liz and Jane
Darby and Laura
Deuce and Puma

Contents

When We Carried Lunchboxes

They say if you remember the 1960s, you weren't really there. But that cliché forgets the actual children of the 1960s; those of us who watched it all unfold, with eyes wide open, imprinted, just like goslings.

We carried psychedelic lunchboxes, wore flowered bellbottoms in size six-x from Healthtex, performed in classroom pageants with theme names like "Feeling Groovy at Holiday Time."

Older teenaged cousins, big sisters in white boots and false eyelashes, long-haired guitar-wielding babysitters, all rolling on the throb of Whiskey A Go Go rock culture and beach be-ins, showed us how to be cool.

My L.A. was Technicolor, a children's playhouse decorated by Disney, the adult world around me increasingly populated by pop stars and ad executives and swingers dressed in paisley ties, white headbands, polka dots, leather minskirts.

The screaming shift from suburban-homeowner tidiness to British-invasion "mod" to full-blown flower power could be seen in every house, playground, garage; tasted and sampled through television ads delivering color-spectrum toys:

Wonder Bread and Twister, with their engorged rainbow dot designs. Screaming Yellow Zonkers, Pink Panther Flakes, Tang, Kool-Aid, green Citrus Cooler Hi-C, everything vibrant and pulsing and coyly and radically named.

We moved from the 8-crayon Crayola box to the 16, then the mighty 64, learning ever more sophisticated nuances from that range: sepia, Burnt Sienna, bronze. The colors of the ages. My dress-up clothes a poison-green party dress. My loungewear: aqua terrycloth.

O aqua! It was everywhere, the flagrant flaming color mood of childhood in L.A., the aqua easy chair (blue leather with brass studs), the aqua Melmac bowl (for taco dip), the Jewish Christmas tree, fake/white, with aqua balls.

Aqua was the crayon that I liked, the eye color of the first girl I approached, the polyester beach pants splotched with tar.

I joined the brainy Aqua reading group and floated in my cousins' aqua pool, watched Aquaman cartoons, stretched out on our rug, my mother spraying Aquanet against her glossy hair.

True elements of aqua hid their faces: oceansurf and sky a murk of haze, dyed & blurry even as we looked to what should have stayed blue under & above.

One caveat of color: we all had to wear "school shoes," in that era before Velcro-fastened sneakers, before Nikes; girls endured the journey up from babyish white saddle shoes to retro red and white, then standard black and white, and then, in fourth grade, came the coveted brown on brown saddle shoes, leather stitched on suede, the variant that every cool girl begged for.

Color dribbled through our growing corporeal systems in the form of medicines: the wet-green Novahistine, off-red Sudafed, bright

Chocks vitamins rattling in our dented Snoopy lunchboxes. Out at
recess, color smacked in puffs from our salmon-pink Voit playballs,
the color you could *smell.*

We clacked our crystal clik-clak balls until they all were banned.
Snapped our hard Bazooka gum, wore the edges off our pink
parallelogram erasers. Back in class, we learned to read in color.
My Little Blue Storybook. My Little Red Storybook. It ended--no
surprise—in that colorless *The Little White House.* Nobody in my
school looked like they lived there. Not even Francisco Villablanca.
In rating us, in ranking, the drag queen sequence of precocious flare
(the SRA reading series) put one kid in Purple, one in Silver.

Orange was the paperback cover of *Harriet the Spy.* Red, white and
blue were all our Bluebird uniforms, our Camp Fire Girl ties, with
scatterings of painted beads sewn on as merit marks.

Everything then sparkled: light on water, show-opening
searchlights, Hollywood's Christmas season blinking out its excess
in the mansions of Beverly Hills stars, the grownups' lava lamps,
our schoolmates' Lite-Brite boards; color TV.

The cracks in the ground. The sidewalk of play, in sand that cups
the hand that cups the sand. The ground that I grew up from
shifted; sank, the ground I grew up from, the up I grew.

Everything orange, golden, groovy, glowing, cheerful, warm. By the
time I had awakened it was 1965; my dad was growing pot down in
our basement; my mother sat beside me on our front steps in L.A.,
discussing why the garbage men were black.

Romantic, 1971

Whither thou goest, I will go. Some have to; some don't get to. That's why my Jewish mother prepares to follow my father to a distant East Coast job; & why I want to stay behind, with my new friend.

The L.A. airport gate: now Mom is weeping; this: her California, wrapped in luggage. Yet I am at a pay phone, dialing (who gave me a dime? It doesn't matter; how'd I get her number? O, she had *mine,* knowing, sensing); I'm dialing up the Cute Girl from my classroom (one year older), saying, "This is it. We're moving. Last chance I have to talk to you."

Curled in that booth, that private phone-space tabletop, me breastless, up against its curve, my family shouting "Bon, we're boarding!"; my mouth open, the last I'll ever speak to her. All of my hallmarks, spilling; romantic, memoir writer; writer. I could have said, "So long, I have to go." Instead I scream "Goodbye forever, and don't forget to write;" and slam it down before she can refuse (refuse to write; deny the invitation).

My mother crying on the jetway; my heart racing—I'm crushed out, dazed. And by the way, I'm ten; bucktoothed, chubby, fake Hawaiian muumuu, "gifted," hopeless; but on that phone, and in my mind, a dashing foreign correspondent; hero to my princess. Exiled, now.

Timberly Drive

In your house it was always spring, when I was a kid. Our thoughts
were barefoot, sunfaced, hot, in soccer t-shirts, overalls rolled up to
square knees. All of us sat legs adangle in your pool; our fingers
shredding dandelions, onion grass, pine needles, leaves, then
jumping to walk warm on dusty wood. Twirling free across a
bedroom floor. Art-stained to our fingertips, handprints on our tie-
dyed faded shorts. Always woods and dogs: something live to run
to. Always spring.

Your house lived forty years after you died. Your ghost sang in the
treebranch pressing on my windowsill, whispering, *I'm out here.*
Come and find me. At first, that branch put spring leaves out to sea
while I was inside scrapbooking your life. As I do every April, now.

Riding on a horse once, your long hair fell in strands like rows of
sticks shiny with kidhood, grave with utter trust. You wrote poems
about riding, and control, and joyful runaway all mixed in round-
inked scrawl that everyone admired. I recall your schoolcoat even
clearer than your freckles: it was beige, blue, brown, all checkered
stiff and soft and warm, as were we all, as kids. You ride some great
horse faster now. Rider, runaway.

Everybody knows you loved me and I loved you, as kids will love,
in plunder, yoyos, secret cigarettes, swapped shirts, admired stories,
nights of laughing, lunchboxes that match, long phone calls.
Playacts. Once you stripped out of your school dress, twirling,
showing off your breasts, your bravery. The last night I ever spent
inside that house, I slept against your restless dreams, your jumps
over the mark, over the love that wouldn't be, or might have

been. Fresh-faced words of fresh-faced boys, my last time there, in the fresh dark, your dresser heavy with the clothes we'd shared and traded; trappings of thirteen-year-olds—records, fat candles, posters, art; old shoes, sex books, ironed batiks, photographs of boys. Of me.

We sat in bed and wrote each other poems, which outlast those sleeps of truth and private jokes; of time, time enough to change our minds.

That house, that yard, that air I breathed, that house as true as schoolroom paper, that house a walk into the world, and many steps learned at eleven.

Walking, there, at twenty-four, without you, even doorknobs ask if spring is back, or whether spring is heaven.

Sunday Ride

That summer was strewn with pines, caked flat with waterfall
boulders; wrapped in an old sheet. That summer was hot with
flavored rice, with dancers in their supplicating poses, soft
formations; pale rain on a Buick windshield, bare feet on the red
canal path. You rolled your rosy limbs into the end of summer,
greening my ache with your light eyes, your fresh-baked sweets,
your breathless laugh, picking your way with ease across the asphalt.

Get in, I said. *We're going for a drive.* Here in the car, a tender,
cupping ride, both of us are bound for our secret battles. Driving
the edge, the strip from outer Baltimore, I'll leave your flannel
kisses there by noon. I'll drive away that song I never liked, and ease
my heart to yours. *Now take the wheel.*

You're driving neatly at the helm, silent and unarmored. Gravel,
trees, a traffic dream of blunders left behind. This car's a journey
anyone can see, a moving, late oasis.

Your open face preserves what is unphotographable; a drive that is
an arrow, shot into the loving arc of humid August. Your open face
shows nothing that is thought but not expressed.

Get out? you asked, in disbelieving proudness. And, hanging damp-
necked from the delicate elbow of the car-door handle, I worked to
keep my cool.

Dance Lesson

Firm chin balanced on cupped left hand, I thrust my old green pen across these lines. These were the hours we met but did not meet; those were the months I wrote but did not write. One long staccato night took me from the barre to stretch to unbound leap and down, damp-fleshed on the hardwood, flexed, turned out. Your eyes followed me, swallowed me; your wood-grained face a consciousness made narrow.

I danced across that worn floor, graceless, careless. A warm space, it encircled us like gnarled tree branches, living, old; I breathed your hands across my back; I knew in you the thoughts of me that lingered. Bent towards some wide future, I met you, halfway, with my bashful heart; bowed to the floor beneath my folded knees.

All Hallow's Eve

Halloween. All Hallow's Eve. The moon is a portentous globule.
This is the ship for death, for witches; these motifs all near at hand.
They come for love, my frightened darling; in this pumpkin glows
your dream.

Death is still that thin veneer of ghostness; and I have my own—
those afternoons where every turn of light and dark, and dust
and tree, conjure you up. Your ghost and I climb slowly down the
basement stairs to that one room shut up, shut off, where we were
once two rustling leaves on the back steps of girlhood. Your death
has been a wisp of smoke now rising as patina, haze, between my
breaths at harvest time. I'm not afraid. This Halloween, my missing
one, come witch upon my distant shore. Our youth, our jack
o'lantern past is ritual enough to burn a candle.

Pipeline

When the pipes burst and blocked and our town was out of water,
we listened to the radio, unwashed. Drank wine, made love, no
need to do the dishes. Our plates accumulated, holy pyres; a night
spent melting ice cubes, toothbrush in a dry glass, bristling; the
dirty river leered, fat with burst pipelines, while we stayed up
recalling the sweet taste of that water we once drank.

Most people live less glibly, and the drought in their own
consciousness is chronic: barren lands, throats tight with thirst are
distant bells, stilled clappers.

When our water flowed back in, I felt I too broke forth, my body
feeding pipelines to the river, knowing life is random. Our town
runs damp again; we have been spared. I found myself disturbed as
from a dream, stumbling to the kitchen, drinking in my sleep.

Two Apartments

Hot.
Chance of late evening cloudbursts.
Insistent mosquitoes dance at the screen.
No worry, love; we are protected
By charms and weather, words and dreams,
Steam rising from the rainspout, memory's kettle
Pressed into our testing of each other.
I am brown in the mirror tonight
Sweat clings to my back
Like varnish to the banister
And the bass is turned up in my spine
The water is warm from the tap tonight,
Spiders sleep on the sill,
Vines wilt over lawns in the fine-smelling dark
My damp shoes dry across yesterday's news
I'm still up, still steaming
Digging my hot fingers
Into the couch
Waiting to hold you
To kiss your long hair
Like hearing the long vines wilt on the lawn
In the fine smelling dark
Awake on the couch
Warm from the tap
Asleep on the still
Steaming up from my shoes
Your hair on my pillow
My heart
In my throat.

Shards

Pain moves in the head like shells in the tide. Like crescent shards
that curl over the drift. You're blanket-wrapped upon the couch,
turned to the walls, perhaps some object in your fist. These static
scenes, conditions, take up all our time.

Awake, alert, you waver between changes, fingers on your pen. In
slumber you are passive. I'm in the rocker writing, waiting; cold
in these distractions, silences.

I never knew you as a girl, or as a whole; I know you in this pond
of your night terrors, where I swim. I am the lifeguard who will not
concede to watch a woman drown tonight.

Some days I live beneath your eyelids rising only in your glance.
My body shudders with your moods. I'm breaking through a
wave that has no nickname, here where you are breathing without
drowning, riding on an even keel at last.

Your Keys

Grieving takes years. Learning your stories took only a night.
Recognition grew from your drinking glass, flipped bottle caps,
keys I still find scattered and suspended, tossed around my
sunroom, winking: listen.

The delicate point of your upper lip against the air that moved as
soft as water, like a tunnel through which comfort rode, quiet as
wool, and close as my own outline: there in that beginning you
were perfect, cautious as anemones and whiskers, fine as grains of
sugar left to linger in the breakfast bowl.

I watched it all; took notes, expecting nothing. I gave no one a
chance to read my mind. I stood up stammering or sat down
telling stories. When it ended, no one but a writer could hear the
pinpoint hammer, the precise line of a boundary, the paragraph
snuffed out like candlewick. I blamed my age, then: born to be
divided, my life halved in two centuries; this one; that.

History

Looking back over that full recent history, looking ahead to
whatever plans I have—or you have—I have reduced hope to the
bare point of simplicity—to the inches between our eyes. The
inches between our noses.

Whatever plans I have lie in the furrows of your squinting laughter,
your bouncing ball of talk, your clenched and joyful fists.

The point of simplicity is a laugh, the turning of your head
to clear your throat, the motion of your hand around a desk-leg.

Whatever plans I have lie in the pattern of our voices playing back
to me, night after night, captured in my aural files, archival history.

We think about the lover we can't see. See the lover we can't live
without.

Cliffside

At daybreak, the late winter whale anchors at the bay, unseen and unwished for. I'm sleeping fast with one rib touching you, one bone's excuse for contact. If you should shift, it wouldn't be to wake me.

Berries drop soundlessly, eaten by dazed geese; this is a quietness unbroken by the awnings scrolling up, the doors pushed out to let in daylight. Old bookshelves creak with unread weight; my notebooks flutter empty. The hour, the whale, the written word share that invisibility, though all three are important.

You move away from me the way a stiff drawer opens—stuttering, shiny; something keeps splintering off; you move toward me like a stiff chair waits, knowing, not approving, the bulk of my intent. Drawer, chair, away and towards, pulling, splintering, we two make a room in disarray, where old women lived, have lived, are living.

At night suitcases close up, swallowing our sandy sneakers. The miles walked by playful feet will vanish in our luggage. We become, again, travelers, mere companions. Not dangerous lovers, not reckless legs and hearts.

A Night on the Sabbath Bed

When I am your Sabbath Queen, I come through your window full
of myself, so full of bearing, caught then, big and laughing, over
the kitchen embers, leaving you blessings where you should find
them.

And on your bed I wear my hair as it once was in childhood, long
for braiding, and you take flowing lumps of it and knot it to your
will. My headskin prickling with desire, hair that stands on end
for you, alive, blood pounding lightly at the nape of my neck.
Then braid me loosely from your amused distance, your adoring
closeness, the noble proximity of your pomegranate breasts that roll
out of the desert in this dream.

From that same tribe we trace our bloodlines back to Egypt where
our dark foremothers shaped the bricks for pharaohs; I see your
Jewish face in mine, a lantern I can walk by. Your history spells my
own in a rough and supple kiss. If once we played as goddesses,
as Sabbath queens, I know in you tonight each spice of that once-
womanly Eden, promised land, weighed and measured, temptingly.
Count them and eat.

Your carob eyes, your chocolate hair, your pale brown skin like
cinnamon; your ginger voice, your nutmeg laugh, your smoky
taste like hazelnuts. Like chicory. Like cardamom. I am a merchant
sampling spice; I am a gardener of delights, a compass point to
seasoning, a table set for holidays. Here on the bed, grind spice for
me, your fingers, lashes, savory skin. Four questions aren't enough
when we are wise and foolish, descendent, first, then ancestor.

Here. Lean back, I remember you: the points of touch are asterisks,
shining in the dark; whether we are parallel, or linear, plotting on a
graph how close we are; how distant.

Climbing out of the bath, earlier, rosy in face and fortune, I bent to
towel your legs dry and waited as you combed your springy head.
I pulled on soft and faded garments, ambling barefoot over the
wood planks of my treehouse; I let myself land like a marlin on the
surface of your old quilt, my damp arms thrown akimbo laughing;
then I pulled you down to kiss your glad eyes with my open mouth.

The moon moved over, one brief glimpse per hour, yellow for
autumn, and I took your head in my long hands and said *Bless me,
Rebekah,* and rocked to the rhythm of your well-known face.

Sounds in the Middle of the Night

One night I made the list of different sounds that woke me while I'd slept beside some women I had loved. My list said *rain,* then *barking dogs,* and grew apace. Hawaiian roosters. Parrots. Garbage trucks, tornado warnings, that flamenco dancer in apartment 309, upstairs, rehearsing. Lightning storms at festivals, your feet racing for shelter, toward me, running. A phone call, once, just teasing me, *don't miss your flight,* knowing I was with somebody else. Your kid in the next room, demanding *what are you women doing?,* too young to understand. That thunder we thought might be bombs falling. We woke up with hearts pounding. The rival who came knocking at your door; I hid, in your old bathrobe. Better, though, the train sounds: distant, holy; so symbolic. The train entered the traffic tunnel, howling. It woke us up. I had to enter you.

Odessa in December

I arrive in the city of my great-grandmother, folded and stamped
as a letter to my ancestors: No, I did not marry, for all that you
endured, that I might do so. Then, in some reverse perverse
migration, I step into these harsh streets with another Jewish girl,
whose reincarnation answers past displacements, our unison an
anthropology.

Here in this port of our inherited bodies we are asking directions,
learning languages, adopting customs, honoring taboos. This primal
search, together, for beginnings ends with memories now frozen
into water.

The oil of matrilineality pooled there. It pooled between our secret,
snow-chapped faces. With just a sigh our faces flamed through days
and nights of Hanukah, the oil of love streaming over planes of
bone, the bridge of our dark eyebrows. We watched two girls who
could be us break ice to open milk cans.

When, finally, she asked me *will we last* I oiled her tender temples
at the hairline, haunted by other women, silenced and now
burning, menorahs seen in winter's window-panes.

The Good Tent

I envy the woods their quiet hours with you, their fibered lives
responding to your questions, the question mark of foliage green
between you. No tree or mountain I might match for eloquence,
the comma of bent boughs and ferns around you. If water were a
woman she might love you. If water were a woman she might
lift her head and look, speak nothing to your quiet as befits this
privacy.

I have gone down to that water, flat grey beneath green brows,
watching the slap of waves up to the boards, watching the
bounding small rabbits and seeing those clouds part like your
hair, inviting, mysterious, pale over dark. Flashing, enveloping,
encircling me, I float, your waterbaby. You create landscapes,
environments: bodies of water, sand dunes, domiciles, and, on land,
our separate two tents. But nothing is too deep for diving here;
water at its deep end carries me.

Cradled in the loving-cup of safety, I tent down before the storm.
Hot thunderheads kiss angrily and split their bellies at the moon.
I'm scared. Thunder so loud and swollen-hearted I am just one of
many creatures, skimming wet, drenched in their burrows,
frantic, waiting. The rain, the night, the wet tent drives me out.
In lightning, storm, in damp and tender cloud light, a great tree
spreads her roots. Her weathers gathered, cloak-like, inviting all to
drink this air, trees nourished, primal, soaking. Everything green
and hot and lush grows faster here, as I grew up, at twenty,
thirty, forty.

It sprang up mushroom-like this time, this thing that happened, liking you, or knowing you, or finding you, when I was wet and scared. Stars and thunder, elements, everything is startling here, clear or heavy, fluid, skin on skin.

Airlift

Her body was a war zone. But in détente, glasnost, perestroika
she became the airlift to Berlin, delivered from this evil empire,
flown across the Iron Curtain, parted for her body journey on the
route as red as her blood vessels, pounding to be fixed, pounding
at Western Europe's door.

When older maps & borders split, her lifeline opened up. A girl
as contraband, or resource, brought by airlift, landing as a peace-
keeping gift bag, landing where designs for master race once
shunned and burned the broken stones paved for Olympiad with
once-rejected bodies.

Now the pace has slowed, the airlift lands, and heads turn to receive
this poet guest who asks no favors, takes her time. Defiant, known,
imperfect.

Geography of Desire

Washington is the city where I came out; where many others have. We first kissed near those very public monuments, transformed into our monuments, our gayness; we marched for gay rights in the same "town" where we lived. Twenty years of being out etched memories where I walked. Bars came and went; gay restaurants, cafes. Yet usually my dating life was elsewhere. I used my city for my working life.

But one time there was someone I liked in my own city at last, after so many long-distance lovers; my own city became my love palace, and the streets where I lived were a geography of desire. The city became a woman when I walked through the streets thinking of her, lost, backtracking.

My neighborhood had grandeur; it had depth. It gained dimensions of her arms and legs, her laughter. I stepped off curbs and crossed streets, thinking of her. The sidewalk was my therapist, answering back "She's not meant to be yours." Cracks where we had leaned were cavewalls, primal drawings. Drugstore fronts where we had hugged were landfalls. I was seasick, lovesick, walking home at night; a tree became important because I looked at it in passing when I loved her.

Like wolves we sprayed desire on every edifice. We marked our turf as casually as that. Doorways, traffic islands, bar stools, lobbies, hallways froze the moments, making architecture remember that I liked her, HERE. THERE. This all came back to haunt me, later; the city was a woman I had longed for, her mark on my own basement wall a taunt. Graffiti tags of challenge lived in cracks upon my rooftop, girl memories in the shifts of urban asphalt, in the trees.

Recklessly, I shopped for gourmet food; I chilled the wine and walked with springlike buoyancy and loved the very pollen on my car. The city was her name upon my mind, my leather jacket smoky, my motions fed with knowing I could run into her. Anywhere. Be ready. Be prepared. I walked out of my door, once, without stopping, to a place where I knew she might be. Our hands brushed on the subway; but tourists noticed nothing. Our bubble of two people had no frame.

We packed it all into one afternoon, one night, packed in like matching luggage. Except that my luggage didn't look like hers when the trip had ended. It all meant something else to me, this trip within my city. Now, walking, driving, everywhere, her words and hands still touch me: on this corner she said those things, there handed me a flower. Individual bricks have their memory of us now. My car seat held her shape for weeks and weeks.

Swimming Lessons

(for Lillian Faderman)

We're walking on the beach when you mention that you never
learned to swim. And me?—I reached up through the curving
overcurl at six and drew the furling lip of wave around me like a
blanket.

Throughout my life I'd sketch the ocean-wave on notebook paper,
cards, my signature; so confident in water, fearless, kicking.

My oceanic childhood was my father, who walked me through
the undertow and showed me how to breathe. (My Jewish mother
watching, terrified.)

In that L.A., when I was six, my swimming lesson season, you were
rising up through waters of your own past without a doting father
to protect you from the riptide, the near drowning.

You rose up on the Venus-shell of learning and surfed your word-
life all the way to shore, then did a stately breaststroke toward long
love.

The afternoon I hold my breath and swim and rush triumphant,
dripping, from a wave, you navigate tsunamis from your past, not
on a surfboard but a mortarboard. It is the year you earn your
doctorate.

You've always kicked your way up to the light, the top part of the
water, glistening and surfaced like a dolphin, with your mind as
graceful as our foremothers in flight who swam the Red Sea, slavery

left behind.

No swimming coach need show you how to dive.
Now history's waves, which you surfed to survive,
break gently at your feet. They sing: *alive.*

The Incident

And this was the incident, sticky as jam. That New Year's Eve I
sat in a living room where I was the only Jew. Chilling out with
my girlfriend and some softball pals of hers all strong and proud,
out and tough; all athletes, educators, ten decent, funny women I
had come to know and love. I'd baked the cookies for their games,
cheering *slide, you got it.*

Then my girlfriend went outside to have a smoke. That was the
moment when I asked a guest named Pam about her work.

"I'm special ed with kids now, but I started as a nanny;" and she
settled in her chair, and I sipped at my martini, and then "But that
first family I worked for? Just the worst. So, I'll tell you," (and I
never saw it coming, like a fast ball pitched at dusk) "because no
one here is Jewish, right?" She looked around. And smiled, with
confidence; for normally, no one would be. They'd all grown up
together, without me. It's just that I was there that night. The Jew
who'd asked to hear about her work.

I felt my right hand fly up like a kitestring, in one swift yanked-up
gesture, waving: *Me! Hey, whoa there! Yes, I'm Jewish. Representing!
Been Jewish all along. Gee, could have sworn you knew!* "Me," I said.
"I'm Jewish." And I dressed it sort of cheery-lite (to mask that
sinking feeling when you know another incident is up.) Sat smiling
with my hand flung up, martini unattended. *Wait! Teacher! Look at
me! Call on me! Take me in! This is the Jew who's cheered you from the
bench.*

But Pam just said, "For real?!" and then continued with the tale

I'd asked to hear. "I'll just call them cheap, then; really cheap," and everybody nodded. There was more? And I looked to the right. Looked to the left. Waiting, as the clock ticked up to twelve.

But no one said, "Shut up, Pam," or, to me, "You know, she didn't mean it," or even the old standby, all my life, the "Oh, no way! But, see, you don't look Jewish." No one thought to ask, "Are you okay?" (Though surely I was all grown up. And hadn't I heard worse?) But no one thought that anything had happened.

It shifted things, beginning then, that night, the differences I tried hard to deny; beginning with *I'm more than just one Jew,* and *You don't know what I do?,* and *I'm on the shelves at New York Public Library.* (The writer ego, quick to take the blow, protecting the soft Semite flesh below.)

But it was New Year's Eve. And my girlfriend missed it all, outside smoking just before the clock struck twelve and everybody kissed. I couldn't say, *So this is how they talk when they're relaxed?* as her face turned, expecting soft lips; *Happy New Year.*

That night was like a fragrant pear which proved to be rock-hard. It disappointed where it looked so sweet. I'm rolling all this out a few years later, on the countertop of memory, pinching it like angry kreplach dough, simmering with what I might have said, and lots of time to think, now that I'm single.

The Dust of Gods and Goddesses

Superbowl Sunday, and I'm missing my dad. Thinking about his dying time, the game we watched, all betting on the Saints. They marched in toward my father, that last time.

And while the city waits, tonight, to rip into the chips and pop the beer, in this cool pregame silence, I am dusting. Dusting round the altar where I keep my father's ashes and some sacred bits. Down on my knees in ski pants for the careful swipe of Pledge around my father.

And it's a mess, the clutter from my travels to the godspots of the world, the goddesspockets. That bottle, steamed with water, holds six ounces from the Amazon; those eagle feathers fell to earth, to forest floor, to me as I sat praying on a stump in Haida nation where I took some ashes, more of dad. It took permission from two Haida carvers. Then a roaring seaplane over islands and seven hours hiking to a tree in a white graveyard where I left dust of my father in a fallen eagles' nest.

Now he can feel the wings that brush the whole Pacific Rim, the oldest growth, the breakaway that tipped the continent, the Haida Gwaii. I dust around the feathers. Then, that bowl.

A bowl of stones from Delos, of Artemis and Isis. A rock that bit my sneaker on a goddess tour. These tiny bits that chafed my shoes, then pebbled in my pocket to take home. And full of dust: so much, I head into the kitchen, to run water on my sacred stones.

I'm laughing. Other households, now, have fans and girlfriends also in the kitchen making up the trays of sacred snacks. Uncorking bottles, ladling out salsa, hovering at ovens puffed with biscuit redolent of game-day manliness. I have to be the only one who's washing goddess rocks. Too late, I see the dirt of ages dribbling in my sink like ordinary coffee grounds, so casual, revealing that one stone I'd never washed before is notched with pattern, ancient overlay: this is a piece of temple floor, a tile. I'm scrubbing with my kitchen spoon, domestic archaeology. My spoon will taste of goddesses forever; though later, when I watch the Super Bowl, the spoon of Isis will contain just hummus. And the game day whistle blares. I'm covered now in dust. My father in my hair, my goddesses.

The tile of Artemis is drying on a paper towel while deep below the city, in the pipes and sewers of this week of snow, of game day, of snot from winter colds, of pregame flushing, and baths of babies and the President, the dust of Artemis is flowing, beating out a pathway to the tidal mouth of river, the lonely voyage eastward back to Delos.

My hands are stained with blessings. Now, I turn to catch the modern gladiators clashing, the spectacle of warriors at play. My house is clean, my hair is filled with history, my father, feathers, Isis stones swept free of modern dust tracked in by me, the living. But in the night, and far below, Potomac water carrying the memories and secrets of our saints.

Lost Needles

She leaves, & leaves a hole in everything, and so, I sew.

Amid my life unraveling, I mend the holes that lie against the skin she is not holding.

Buttons hanging loose, as I am, hurting, my whole soul a pricked finger, threadbare, ripped, my feelings, fingertips, my buttonholes.

Then I lose the needle, poking in the red pincushion heart. The round old sawdust heart I've had in every place I've lived in where I've loved. And, feeling like an animal, a murderer, a failure (can't even find a *needle* in the *haystack* of my life), I cut the pincushion open, spill its guts into a bowl to get my needle (& my girlfriend) back.

Through all these years, I never thought to look, to see how many needles I had lost (For what's a needle? Not like a lost woman.) But now, tonight, red sawdust in the bowl explodes with needles, long, and short, and small from every home I ever had where buttons loosened, or pajamas split. I lost a pack of needles through the years.

Confronted, now, at fifty, with the sting of everyone who left the hurt I buried deep (& didn't find) all of an evening, spilled out like a tear, these needles—my lost lovers—in a bowl.

Mercy Ledge

I read her face at first sight, deep as chapters. She is my book, & she
is reading me, & I am novel. I am perfect bound. I am softcover,
turning, turning. Turning. Typset in my change of life, I find my
reader, reading with one eye. Mercy, do I know this edge, this
seafront-slippery precipice; this point where lava stops its flow and
sneakers start to stick. Mercy, as I walk out to that edge and plant
the flags that mark our boundary.

Beach Glass

Up until then I had always been young. That was all I'd ever known, the youngest, the achiever, skipped ahead. Then I became a grownup, past precocious, as awkward as a colt. Heading into menopause, walking on life's beaches, finding glass.

Yes, this is about beach glass. It washes up and waits to be collected. I fill up jars, and bowls, and sandy baskets. This is a my symbol of redemption, hope, repair; restorative justice, if you like. Something sharp and broken, ruined, painful, goes flying out to sea and comes back art. The ocean smoothes its edges, heals, reforms.

There was a year of cringing, an ice cube tray of small humiliations. A big misunderstanding, and I had to make amends, cringe and be so careful, a belly-up small timberwolf on cautious sorry paws. But anguish became beach glass: I learned the ways of meaning I was sorry. What went wrong floated back to us, as beach glass does. And sometimes, lover, we wash up upon each others' beach towels, as art not perfect and quite far from finished.

I found your jagged edges: come back to me as beach glass, better polished. Where beauty has no broken edge to it, the Goddess runs her thumb over us all.

About the Author

Bonnie J. Morris is an emeritus professor of women's studies and women's history and the author of seventeen other books; she has taught at Harvard Divinity School, George Washington University, Georgetown University, UC-Berkeley, and on three global voyages for Semester at Sea. A 2017 recipient of a Ruth Rowan Believer Award from the National Women's Music Festival, she is the archivist for Olivia Records and organized the first-ever exhibit of women's music and lesbian recordings at the Library of Congress. Find her at www.bonniejmorris.com

Acknowledgments

Many thanks to the editors of the following publications, in which these poems appeared, sometimes in earlier versions:

all things jezbian: "The Incident"

Nimrod Awards 3: "Dust of Gods and Goddesses"

Sinister Wisdom: "The Incident"

The Gay and Lesbian Review: "Cliffside"

Word of Mouth: 150 Short-short Stories by 90 Women Writers,
      ed. Irene Zahava: "Pipeline" (as "Water Geographies")

Headmistress Press Books

Demoted Planet - Katherine Fallon

Earlier Households - Bonnie J. Morris

The Things We Bring with Us: Travel Poems - S.G. Huerta

The Water Between Us - Gillian Ebersole

Discomfort - Sarah Caulfield

The History of a Voice - Jessica Jopp

I Wish My Father - Lesléa Newman

Tender Age - Luiza Flynn-Goodlett

Low-water's Edge - Jean A. Kingsley

Routine Bloodwork - Colleen McKee

Queer Hagiographies - Audra Puchalski

Why I Never Finished My Dissertation - Laura Foley

The Princess of Pain - Carolyn Gage & Sudie Rakusin

Seed - Janice Gould

Riding with Anne Sexton - Jen Rouse

Spoiled Meat - Nicole Santalucia

Cake - Jen Rouse

The Salt and the Song - Virginia Petrucci

mad girl's crush tweet - summer jade leavitt

Saturn coming out of its Retrograde - Briana Roldan

i am this girl - gina marie bernard

Week/End - Sarah Duncan

My Girl's Green Jacket - Mary Meriam

Nuts in Nutland - Mary Meriam & Hannah Barrett

Lovely - Lesléa Newman

Teeth & Teeth - Robin Reagler

How Distant the City - Freesia McKee

Shopgirls - Marissa Higgins

Riddle - Diane Fortney

When She Woke She Was an Open Field - Hilary Brown

A Crown of Violets - Renée Vivien tr. Samantha Pious

Fireworks in the Graveyard - Joy Ladin
Social Dance - Carolyn Boll
The Force of Gratitude - Janice Gould
Spine - Sarah Caulfield
I Wore the Only Garden I've Ever Grown - Kathryn Leland
Diatribe from the Library - Farrell Greenwald Brenner
Blind Girl Grunt - Constance Merritt
Acid and Tender - Jen Rouse
Beautiful Machinery - Wendy DeGroat
Odd Mercy - Gail Thomas
The Great Scissor Hunt - Jessica K. Hylton
A Bracelet of Honeybees - Lynn Strongin
Whirlwind @ Lesbos - Risa Denenberg
The Body's Alphabet - Ann Tweedy
First name Barbie last name Doll - Maureen Bocka
Heaven to Me - Abe Louise Young
Sticky - Carter Steinmann
Tiger Laughs When You Push - Ruth Lehrer
Night Ringing - Laura Foley
Paper Cranes - Dinah Dietrich
On Loving a Saudi Girl - Carina Yun
The Burn Poems - Lynn Strongin
I Carry My Mother - Lesléa Newman
Distant Music - Joan Annsfire
The Awful Suicidal Swans - Flower Conroy
Joy Street - Laura Foley
Chiaroscuro Kisses - G.L. Morrison
The Lillian Trilogy - Mary Meriam
Lady of the Moon - Amy Lowell, Lillian Faderman, Mary Meriam
Irresistible Sonnets - ed. Mary Meriam
Lavender Review - ed. Mary Meriam